GEHRY

Design Monographs

Design Monographs

GEHRY

NAOMI STUNGO

Frank Gehry | There are few buildings that people will cross the world to see. The Taj Mahal, the Pyramids, the Parthenon, maybe. Frank Gehry's Guggenheim Museum in Bilbao is one such. In the two years following its opening in 1997, more than two million visitors poured into the northern Spanish city whose principle – some would say only – attraction the museum is. Featured in countless newspapers, colour supplements and fashion magazine, Gehry's astonishing building put Bilbao on the map – so much so that the city's airport had to expand to keep up with the demand – and confirmed Gehry's position as the world's most famous living architect.

"The museum in Bilbao leads to a new era in building," said British architect Norman Foster at the time of the Guggenheim's opening. Gehry's friend, the sculptor Richard Serra, has claimed that "Frank represents a break with all contemporary architecture. His is not an architecture that arises from an older order. He is the first really to break with the orthodoxy of the right angle."

In reality, Gehry's Guggenheim Museum is just the most public of a long string of unorthodox buildings. Since setting up his own practice in Los Angeles in the early 1960s, Gehry's work has consistently challenged the conventions of what a building should look like. His work has ripped apart the idea of a building as a box-like container comprising four walls at right angles to each other, a roof and a floor, replacing it instead with something altogether more fluid. The wild exuberance of the Guggenheim is simply the logical product of this process.

Gehry's buildings have created a new paradigm for architecture, one that critics Peter Arnell and Ted Bickford refer to as a "new perspective".

What is truly striking is the public's acceptance of this idea. For some reason Gehry's architecture is not seen as "difficult" in the way much modern

Opposite. Guggenheim Museum Bilbao, 1997.

art is. Quite the contrary, the public flock to see his buildings, as witnessed by the popularity of the Guggenheim in Bilbao.

In much the same way that Cubist artists at the beginning of the twentieth century shattered the single-point perspective on which western art was founded, Gehry's architecture at the end of the century presented buildings as an astonishing clash. An all-angles-at-once experience.

It has taken a while, however, for Gehry to reach this position. He has now been designing strange-looking buildings for nearly three-quarters of a century. Born in Toronto in 1929, he likes to describe how his grandmother encouraged his boyhood interest in architecture by helping him to make weird little structures out of scraps of wood. Part of Gehry's strength as a designer, however, comes from the fact that he is not just interested in architecture. As important an influence on his later professional development was his mother, who took the young Frank to Toronto's art galleries, helping to foster his life-long love of painting and sculpture.

Gehry was eighteen when the family uprooted, leaving the familiarity of Toronto for sprawling Los Angeles. The move, Gehry later acknowledged, was an enormous upheaval that left him both overwhelmed and fascinated by his new environment. Confused and unsure of himself, Gehry eventually enrolled at the University of Southern California to study, not architecture but fine art.

The discovery of architecture took a while. One of Gehry's classes at USC was a ceramics course taught by Glen Lukens. Lukens took an interest in Gehry and invited him round to his house to meet Raphael Soriano, the architect whom he had commissioned to design his new place. The meeting, Gehry says, left him "lit up".

"I had just come from Canada and I didn't know anything and it was a bad time. My father had lost everything. I was really on the floor with lack of self-esteem. Not knowing what I wanted to do when I was seventeen or eighteen, I had started working as a truck driver and I was fascinated with people who did know what to do. I was looking for a model, I guess," he recalled in discussion with Kurt Forster.

The effect of the meeting with Soriano was obvious to Lukens, who suggested to Gehry that he might enjoy studying architecture. Gehry started night classes in the architecture department. "I did really well," he says. "It was my first connection to something. They skipped me to the second year. It was a big deal." And yet, even so, Gehry had not quite found himself. He was constantly pushing at the system and testing its limits, dreaming up joint projects with the art department that, given the thoroughly traditional nature of the university, were invariably rejected.

Trying a different approach, Gehry began post-graduate studies in city planning at Harvard in 1956. He hated it and dropped out before the year ended. To fill his time, he did odd jobs and took a number of courses, including one taught by Joseph Hudnut, an architect and writer. Instead of lecturing on classical architecture in a darkened amphitheatre, Hudnut took his students on walking tours of Boston, discussing with them its "American" architecture – the city's terraced (or "row") houses, industrial buildings and other vernacular architecture.

The experience had a huge impact on Gehry. "It gave me something to strive for: creating an American architecture," he explains. "After all, I was in America, I should make American architecture. And that meant that you had to find a new language because one didn't really exist yet. It existed in the way he explained it, but the game was to find a new one."

Making your way in architecture is slow business, though. Married by now and with a family to support, Gehry moved back to California in the late 1950s and started work as an architect, first in the office of Victor Gruen and eventually on his own. It was to be twenty years before he achieved any real fame. In the meantime, he set about developing his contacts in the art world. Los Angeles had a vigorous artistic community. Making friends with a number of leading artists, sculptors and designers, Gehry gradually got commissions that, at last, helped him bridge the art and architecture divide. Little by little, Gehry started to develop his own, very distinctively new architectural language.

His first notable project was a house and studio for graphic designer Louis Danziger and his wife Dorothy on a busy corner in Hollywood. The Danziger Studio and Residence (1964–65) took its cue both from the industrial and commercial flavour of the neighbourhood and from minimalist sculpture.

Adopting the simple, cube-like form of cheap commercial buildings in the area, Gehry created two linked volumes: one for the studio, the other for

Above left. Danziger Studio and Residence, 1965. **Above right.** O'Neill Hay Barn, 1968.

the house. The drama came from the relationship between the two. Gehry has explained, "I was ... interested in the idea of connection, of putting pieces together, in a way very similar to what I am still doing twenty years later. I suppose we only have one idea in our lives."

Like the Danziger Studio and Residence, the O'Neill Hay Barn in San Juan Capistrano, California (1968), drew heavily on contemporary sculpture. The barn – part of a larger master plan for a new ranch with stables, guest house and additional buildings – was a simple structure: a huge roof and skirt of corrugated iron supported on wood posts. But by tilting the roof, Gehry gave the building a dashing abstract quality reminiscent of works by sculptors such as Carl Andre and Donald Judd.

It was after seeing the Hay Barn that the painter Ron Davis asked Gehry to design him a house in Malibu (1972). The commission proved an important one for Gehry, enabling him to achieve what he had so long striven for – to establish a collaborative relationship with an artist. Lengthy discussion with Davis on perspective, geometry and illusion seemed to free up Gehry's imagination. The result was a house that broke with the conventions of the orthogonal box to a greater extent than ever before: a rhomboidal construction with a steeply tilting roof which focused visitors' attentions on the building's vanishing point, the nearby lake.

"I was nervous about that project," Gehry admitted long after it was built. "I thought the degree of the angles might be bizarre and make you feel uneasy. In fact, it was very restful. The building unlocked a whole lot of other possibilities for me. I spent a lot of time there, sitting and looking for a lot of days and evenings, watching the reflections. That helped me in my house. Because nothing was parallel, you couldn't predict where the shadows and sunlight and reflections would fall. If you've got a straight rectangular box with rectangular windows, you sense where these things come from. But if things aren't all straight, then you get a different take. That's become an interesting part of my work."

At different points throughout his career, collaborating with artists has helped Gehry to unlock ideas, to move from one stage to the next, but it would be wrong to see his work as pure art. Gehry considers himself to be first and foremost an architect. He designs buildings that function, that have gutters and drains and all the paraphernalia of real, serviceable buildings.

And yet what is so striking about his work is that he plays with the materials of architecture much as a painter or sculptor experiments with paint or clay. "There's an immediacy in paintings," he says. "You feel like the brush strokes were just made ... I wanted to see what else we can learn from paintings. In particular, how could a building be made to look like it's in process?"

As his architecture gradually loosened up, Gehry increasingly accentuated the process by which he constructed his buildings, emphasizing the very timber, corrugated iron, chain-link fencing and so on from which they were assembled.

With these ideas in mind, Gehry set about converting his own house. His remodelling of the pink, two-storey, 1920s shingle house in Santa Monica established his reputation as one of the most provocative architects of the day.

Gehry once said that he never wanted to design "pretty" buildings. "I don't look for the soft stuff, the pretty stuff. It puts me off because it seems unreal.

I have this socialistic or liberal attitude about people and politics: I think of the starving kids and that do-gooder stuff I was raised on. So a pretty little salon with the beautiful colours seems like a chocolate sundae to me. It's too pretty. It's not dealing with reality. I see reality as harsher; people bite each other. My take on things comes from that point of view."

Within five years of the Santa Monica house's remodelling, 70 per cent of Gehry's neighbours had moved away. It is not hard to see why: the Gehry Residence (1978) is a seriously harsh house. Using the rough and ready materials of the building site – corrugated iron, plywood and chain-link fencing – Gehry wrapped the exterior of the house in a new skin, an awkward angular jarring layer behind which the remnants of the "pretty" original could still be seen.

"I was concerned with maintaining a 'freshness' in the house," Gehry said. "Often this freshness is lost – in over-finishing [houses], their vitality is lost. I wanted to avoid this by emphasizing the feeling that the details are still in process: that the building hasn't stopped. The very finished building has security and it's predictable. I wanted to try something different. I like playing at the edge of disaster."

Adding this unfinished-looking new layer to the outside of the house, Gehry stripped the original house back to its skeleton so that it, too, looked as if it were still in the process of being made. He took the plaster off most of the original walls, leaving just bare stud-and-lath partitions and ripped out the entire upstairs ceiling to expose the redwood roof rafters and create an enormous attic storey. Playing games with left-over pieces of the old house, he embodied them in the new design in utterly incongruous ways – an old sash window was reused as a medicine cabinet, for instance.

The neighbours may not have liked it, but the Gehry Residence marked a turning point in Gehry's career. Its benefits were slow to be felt, however. "It freaked out my developer clients," Gehry explains. "They said, 'If you like that, you don't want to deal with our stuff.'" Today, he acknowledges that they were probably right. At the time, it meant that he had to start out all over again.

Gradually, however, Gehry did find clients who responded to his new-found style. By the late 1970s, disenchantment with modernism was growing and an increasing number of both architects and patrons were looking for something new. Gehry's iconoclastic style was a fresh take, a radical rethinking of what architecture could be.

Gehry has never been afraid of trying out new ideas and styles. Indeed, one of the things that characterizes his work is his willingness to junk tried-and-tested ideas and to invent new ones.

To start with, commissions were, admittedly, pretty small-scale: the odd house or small housing complex, some exhibition design work. Gradually, larger projects materialized. One of the most significant was the scheme to design a new master plan for the Loyola Law School in Los Angeles, a project that was to last, on and off, for much of the next twenty years.

Below. Gehry Residence, 1994.

Gehry's buildings at Loyola (1978–2002) seem to mark an abrupt change from the rough-and-ready "wood butcher" look of the Gehry Residence. In part, they do. The corrugated iron and weird angles are gone, replaced by fresh, stuccoed walls painted in cheerful colours.

At Loyola, a new style was appropriate: a university campus called for a less confrontational approach and, besides, the part of Los Angeles where Loyola was established was tough enough as it was without adding challenging, difficult architecture.

At another level, though, there are strong similarities between Gehry's approach at Loyola and at his own home: undercurrents that run throughout all his work, providing on-going links despite the endless changes in style.

It is easy to see why Gehry had thought he would enjoy urban design. You only have to look at his work to see his fascination with the way people move about cities and spaces, with the way buildings relate to one another. Discouraged by his experience at Harvard, he never pursued urbanism on a large scale. Instead, he has developed his ideas on a micro level – in his buildings. Very rarely, if ever, does he design a monolithic building. Instead, as he did at Loyola, Gehry tends to break projects down into a number of discrete parts, even discrete buildings, which he then links together as though they are separate buildings in a city.

In butchering his house and adding a new layer to it, Gehry created a new and unusual landscape of routes and passageways linking spaces. At Loyola he gradually developed a whole new campus, designing a string of new buildings. As important as the buildings, however, were the spaces he created between them. With its new faculties, squares and pathways, it was a city in miniature.

With the California Aerospace Museum and Theater (1982–84), Gehry again broke the building down into different parts. But here he did what he so often does: he created two completely different-shaped buildings and clapped them together, bolting a metal-clad, seven-sided polygon on to a pale, stone-covered rectangular building to create dramatic volume. In much the

Opposite above. Loyola Law School, 1980. **Opposite below.** California Aerospace Museum and Theater, 1984.

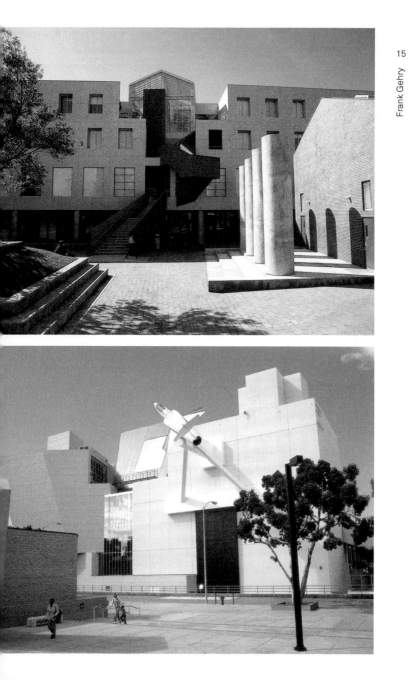

same way that hot-dog stands in America often have a huge hot-dog advertising sign, Gehry whacked a Lockheed F-104 aeroplane over the entrance, just in case there was any confusion over what the building housed.

Gehry was gradually getting bigger and bigger commissions; clients were starting to seek him out precisely because of his unusual style. Even so, he continued to design small, one-off houses.

Houses seem to be a test-bed for Gehry, the place where many of his ideas get refined. The results are often pretty unusual. Take the Norton Residence in Venice, California (1982–84), a building Gehry referred to as his "pride and joy". Instead of putting the house on the (admittedly rather noisy) beachfront, Gehry placed it at the back of the long narrow lot, creating a raised observation deck for his client – who had started out as a lifeguard – at the front of the site with direct views above the traffic over the ocean.

At the Winton Guest House in Wayzata, Minnesota (1982–87), Gehry started playing with different building materials. The project, which was commissioned by a couple who lived in a 1950s Philip Johnson house, was a considered response to Johnson's sleek, steel-and-glass pavilion.

Creating a collection of differently shaped volumes, he clad each room in a different material – Finnish plywood, galvanized metal, brick, stone, painted metal panels. It was the start of a fascination with materials that would lead, via an unbuilt house for Peter Lewis (1989–95), to the titanium cladding of the Guggenheim Museum.

By the mid-1980s, Gehry had achieved huge success – the kind of success that allows you to start doing what you want to do. With the Chiat/Day Building (1985–91), the headquarters of the West Coast advertising company, he teamed up with his friends, the artists Claes Oldenburg and Coosje van Bruggen, to create a building in which art and architecture were each as important as the other. Anyone entering the three-storey building in Venice, California, has first to negotiate Oldenburg's giant binoculars – a huge sculpture that forms the building's entrance and houses conference and research spaces.

The building was a massive logo for both Chiat/Day and Gehry. Hugely arresting, it was reproduced in countless magazines around the world. It is no surprise that, not long afterwards, Gehry won a string of foreign commissions.

Gehry has designed two complexes for the Vitra furniture company, one in Weil am Rhein in Germany, the other in Basel in Switzerland. The first, a furniture-manufacturing facility and design museum (1987–89), marked an important transition: a move away from angular, geometric forms towards a much more fluid, curvaceous architecture. Always one for a pithy label, the critic Charles Jencks dubbed Gehry's new style "vermiform". The museum, in particular, is an astonishing whirling dervish creation: an explosion of energy and shapes, of curving white walls and rakish titanium-zinc-covered roof lights that bring daylight flooding into the building's interior. Gehry developed this fluidity further at the headquarters he designed for Vitra in Basel (1988–94). Here the building is so fluid that it looks as though it was carved in ice cream that has gently melted.

By the early 1990s, Gehry's architecture was getting amazingly complicated to build. His Santa Monica studio was littered with endless cardboard models and reams of blueprints as he and his staff developed ever more complex forms and then tried to figure out how to build them.

When Gehry decided that the solution to a commission to design a retail centre for the Barcelona Olympic Village (1989–92) was to create a mall with a 49-metre (160-foot) long and 30-metre (100-foot) tall sculpture of a fish on top, the practice had really set themselves a tough design challenge. The budget was tight, the schedule tighter still. The only answer was to move to using computer-aided design software.

After extensive research, the practice eventually plumped for a French package – CATIA (Computer-Aided Three-Dimensional Interactive Application) – developed by the aeronautics industry and used to design the Mirage fighter jet. The advantage of the program was that it allowed highly complex forms to be modelled. Simply by running a laser pen, similar to those used by a brain surgeon, over the surface of the cardboard models, their coordinates were mapped into the computer which then created the building's skeleton and calculated the components so accurately that, even if every single piece was differently shaped, the whole thing just fit together like a jigsaw puzzle on site. It is this technology that had enabled Gehry – or otherwise his 120-strong staff, as he has never learned to use a computer – to design ever more astonishing forms.

Gehry is first and foremost an architect, but it would be wrong to think that his interest in creating unusual shapes extended only to buildings. Like many other architects, he has also designed furniture. Back in the late 1960s, he began experimenting with cheap materials, bending and moulding them into furniture. The result was a series of chairs, tables, chaises longues and bed frames made from cardboard. Originally selling for between $15 and $115, they have since become collector's items.

Always restless, always looking at materials and trying to figure out new ways of using them, Gehry returned to furniture-making in the late 1980s, this time using thin strips of laminate redwood that he wove together to make ultra-lightweight chairs and table frames. These have become much coveted. Visitors to the Guggenheim Museum can try them out in the cafeteria.

The Guggenheim Museum in Bilbao (1991–97) was by far Gehry's best-known building by the turn of the century. The museum transformed the Basque capital from a post-industrial wasteland into an international tourist destination. It has proved so popular that, in its first year, ticket revenue represented 0.5 per cent of the Basque region's GDP.

When Gehry first saw the site for the museum – a run-down strip of land right in the city centre alongside the Nervión river – he realized this building needed to be both a response to the city and a dynamic new interjection into it. His competition-winning design is an astonishing building like no other: an explosion on the waterfront, a riot of tumbling shapes and forms. If it resembles anything at all, it is perhaps an enormous cargo ship or battleship. Either would be appropriate. Bilbao was traditionally the heart of the Spanish steel industry and a vigorous port. The building's titanium cladding is meant to be a sort of "memory" of this heritage as well as a beautiful, polished finish that reflects what sunlight there is in Spain's wettest region.

The building turned Gehry into an international celebrity. He became the architect that cities and organizations wanted. A Frank Gehry building is considered something that adds huge cachet to a place or a brand. Over the years, institutions as conservative as banks have commissioned him – he designed the Nationale-Nederlanden Building in Prague (1992–96) – as have

Opposite above. Bentwood chairs for Knoll, 1992, in the workshop studio. **Opposite below.** Snake lamp for New City Editions, 1989.

The only reason to do more expressive buildings is to humanize them. Dull glass boxes are cold and not friendly to humanity and I am trying to change some of that.
Frank Gehry, interview with *Euronews*, 2014

cities reinventing themselves for the twenty-first century – he finished a headquarters building in Pariser Platz in Berlin (1994–2000).

Gehry has continued to challenge conventions and to reinvent himself. One of the most unusual projects to arrive on his drawing board was neither a headquarters for a multi-national corporation nor a new cultural institution. In 1999, he announced that he would design – for free – two cancer-care centres in Britain in memory of his friend, the landscape architect Maggie Keswick Jencks, wife of the critic Charles Jencks. She had died of breast cancer in 1996, but not before setting up a day-care centre for other cancer sufferers at Edinburgh's Western General Hospital. It represented Gehry's first commission in the UK.

Design work began on the Dundee centre with a shoestring budget of an initial £300,000, making the project a real challenge. Gehry readily acknowledged, "We are going to have to get 'the most bangs for the buck'," but then that is what he is so very good at.

When it was unveiled in 2003, the understated, homely construction elicited warm praise. The two-storey structure with an elliptical tower is painted white, and topped off with a crinkled, stainless-steel roof that was inspired by the pleats in a portrait by Vermeer. The overall structure was

Opposite. Wiggle chair for Vitra, 1972.

I'm an egomaniac like all the others, but I'm a Canadian egomaniac. Modesty is built into our lives.
Frank Gehry

influenced by traditional Scottish architecture, having something of a "but and ben" (basic two-room cottage) and broch (prehistoric hollow dwelling) about it. The centre offers oncology patients a space for rest, reflection and counselling. It overlooks the Tay Estuary (intriguingly, Gehry initially imagined it as a small lighthouse) and is set in a garden designed by Arabella Lennox-Boyd that also features an Antony Gormley sculpture. Ten years later, Gehry's second Maggie's opened in Hong Kong; its landscaper was Maggie Jencks's daughter, Lily. There are now 23 centres in the UK and abroad.

For all its undoubted triumph (both in architectural and economic terms), Gehry's Guggenheim bequeathed a controversial legacy, summed up in the term "Bilbao effect". It heralded an era of high-budget, startlingly unconventional projects in architecture, frequently built in the hope of boosting tourism to revive a flagging local economy. Witness Gehry's design for the Marqués de Riscal in Elciego, Spain (2003–06) – his first hotel – which boasted folded canopies of titanium and silver (offering welcome shade from the strong sunlight), their warm hues complementing the Rioja wines grown in the vineyards below. It revitalized both the winery, which had remained largely the same since its foundation in 1858, and the surrounding region.

Gehry's Experience Music Project (1995–2000) in Seattle (renamed the Museum of Pop Culture in 2016) displayed the vibrant, curvilinear metallic surfaces that had become a Gehry trademark since at least the swooping roofs of the Vitra Design Museum, though here in an iridescent array of colours. Given Gehry's propensity for working intuitively, it's no accident that he has compared his approach to that of jazz musicians. In one telling example, he cited improv saxophonist Wayne Shorter's response when some sessions musicians asked him about rehearsals: "You can't practise what you ain't already invented."

Early on in the process, Gehry reportedly sliced up some electric guitars and reconfigured their parts into a prototype model – an approach entirely in keeping with the theme of the museum itself, but also by now inherent to his liberating designs.

The project once again employed computer-generated 3D models, created with Dassault Systèmes' CATIA software. Granted, it had enabled Gehry's office to come up with design solutions that had hitherto been unworkable, but the approach has been criticized too, for prioritizing spectacular form over prosaic function. The price paid for the liquid lines and organic curves of such buildings – which have earned the somewhat pejorative epithet "blobitecture" – can be a standalone building that exists in isolation from its milieu, which could be transplanted to a host of sites worldwide and work equally well (or poorly) there. In 2015, Peter Buchanan savaged both Gehry and Zaha Hadid on these grounds, arguing: "Both arrogantly flaunt their refusal to defer to local context and its codes."

At their least inspired, such outsized curiosities seemed to be ostentatious for their own sake, showy "starchitecture" practised by "starchitects". Both terms have been levelled at Gehry himself, much to his annoyance: at a press conference in 2014, he notoriously responded to the implication by elevating his middle finger. Another of Gehry's more prominent naysayers, art critic Hal Foster, has also taken the architect to task on this point, and for allowing personal expression too great a say in his work, while also criticizing the extent to which Gehry's signature style dominates his projects, reducing them to more-or-less interchangeable "logotecture". On the same note, Foster has also referred to a "disconnection between skin and structure [a building's exterior and interior] that one often senses in Gehry".

Any argument for the defence would surely include the architect's design for the Walt Disney Concert Hall in California (1999–2003) – an aesthetic sibling to the Bilbao Guggenheim (which it actually predates in terms of design), with sweeping, sail-like forms that might also suggest music in full flow, or the bustle of a city's streets. Hal Foster's criticism of an internal/ external disconnect holds no water here, as the auditorium is topped by a

Above. Walt Disney Concert Hall, 2003.

single expanse of steel roof, curved both to improve acoustics and to complement the shape of the outside of the building. The exquisite sound quality of the auditorium was the result of a three-way collaboration with master acoustician Yasuhisa Toyota and conductor Esa-Pekka Salonen, then music director for the Los Angeles Philharmonic, the hall's home orchestra. Salonen also contributed to an architectural plan that sees musicians and audience joined together in one non-hierarchical space – spectators circling the performance area, and with no boxes or other partitions.

Still, Foster wasn't alone in his suspicions about Gehry's supposed excesses. The architect had actually been dismissed from the project in 1994 and it took time for him to bring the clients and financiers around (it also wound up becoming one of the very few of his projects to exceed its budget).

Then again, Gehry has become a specialist at defying expectations. A passing glance at the Cleveland Clinic Lou Ruvo Center for Brain Health (2007–10) might seem to justify his critics' barbs. Set at an intersection in downtown Las Vegas, it comprises two buildings – joined by a steel trellis.

By far the most striking of the pair is the activity centre, a twisted sprawl of metal surfaces, seemingly caught in mid-collapse, dotted with windows or window-like shapes. Yet its arrestingly off-kilter appearance is one of its unique selling points, serving to draw inquisitive onlookers in, where they discover an institution dedicated to research into Alzheimer's and Huntington's disease (the second building, comprising stacked boxes, houses research facilities and clinics). "For me, architecture was a necessary marketing tool," Ruvo told *Architect* magazine. "We wanted a statement that would show we were serious about curing a disease and would let the doctors know we were not underfunded." The architecture helped spotlight the work of the centre; the activity centre helped raise funds as a space for events. And in this case, the Gehry signature certainly played its part.

Completed that same year (but officially opened in 2011), Gehry's stunning design for 8 Spruce Street in New York – his first skyscraper – demonstrated a wholehearted sensitivity to its setting. It had to: the 76-storey, glass-and-stainless-steel edifice had Cass Gilbert's neo-Gothic Woolworth Building (1913) for a neighbour. A wave of drape-like undulations on three of its sides gives the building's façade its unmistakable identity, allowing its surfaces to respond to shifting light and weather patterns. Fashioned from some 10,500 separate shaped-metal panels, its rippled texture (which shares common ground both with Opus Hong Kong, completed in 2012, and Gehry's residential apartments near London's Battersea Power Station, 2022) adds animation and pizzazz to the skyline of a city that was built on those qualities, actually justifying the chutzpah of its alias title "New York by Gehry".

And if its flat top comes as a surprise, given the glamorous twists along its height (no spire or similar architectural exclamation mark to crown it off?), that

When you talk to New Yorkers ... you want to show them something like Bernini or Picasso.
Frank Gehry, *The Guardian*, 2011

was a deliberate choice. "I toyed with the thing," Gehry admitted to *The Guardian* in 2011, "but it ended up looking pretty trivial, trying too hard to be something, against the Woolworth Building. I have too much respect for the Woolworth Building to do a hoopty-do thing." Even the bay windows that project out from 8 Spruce Street's rippled heights nod to Gilbert's iconic building: they are the same scale as the Woolworth's terracotta panels.

Praise for Gehry's achievement was nigh-on unanimous. Doubtless he would have particularly cherished the review by Paul Goldberger of *The New Yorker*, who welcomed it as "the first thing built downtown since [the Woolworth Building in 1913] that actually deserves to stand beside it."

As with many of Gehry's projects, the inspiration for the façade's eye-catching twists and ripples came from Renaissance artists. The sharp folds in the sculptures of Gian Lorenzo Bernini gave the architect a 3 am "eureka" moment, encouraging him to dispense with the more rounded forms he'd originally envisaged and opt for something (literally) edgier. It's another reminder that fine art was Gehry's first love and continues to be a muse; as late as 2021, he was telling *The Art Newspaper* that "I have always been interested in how light hits buildings and in capturing a very painterly 'brush stroke' in my buildings." And tellingly, the commendation he received along with the prestigious Pritzker Architecture Prize in 1989 praised his "sophisticated and adventurous aesthetic that emphasizes the art of architecture". Each project still starts with Gehry's highly gestural, energetic scribbles, which – despite their tendency towards abstraction – more often than not bear a startling resemblance to the completed building.

All of which gave his redesign of the Art Gallery of Ontario (2004–08) – in Gehry's hometown of Toronto, to boot – extra emotional resonance. It was a hands-down success: an elegant and restrained reimagining that created a welcoming, easy-to-navigate environment, with a glass-and-timber frontage that strikes a note of panache (its two ends appear to be lifting away from the centre) without overreaching itself. The second-floor Galleria Italia promenade, which runs the full length of that front, has something of a ship's frame about it, or of a whale's belly, thanks to its curved Douglas-fir timbers,

Opposite. 8 Spruce Street – Gehry's first skyscraper, 2011.

All the great painters of the Renaissance were also architects, from Giotto to El Greco.
Frank Gehry, interview with *Financial Times*, 2022

and prompted *The Wall Street Journal* to claim it as "Toronto's finest interior space". Both the Galleria and a striking spiral staircase provide new views on to the city. The project ticked all the boxes for practicality too, doubling the exhibition space, ensuring all the galleries were well lit, and staying within both the building's footprint and the $276-million budget.

Gehry brought many of his signature touches together for the Fondation Louis Vuitton (2014) art museum in Paris, not least the twelve huge glass sail-like forms (comprising 3,584 uniquely curved laminated glass panels, for which a special furnace had to be constructed). Commissioned by Bernard Arnault, founder of the luxury-goods conglomerate LVMH and the richest man in France, it stands near the city's Bois de Boulogne. Gehry studied the use of glass and metal in nineteenth-century garden architecture, notably the Beaux-Arts Grand Palais on the Champs-Élysées, and the Palmarium in the nearby Jardin d'Acclimatation, a children's park. The "sails" fly above eleven galleries, housed in white concrete blocks that led Gehry to dub them "icebergs", along with a 350-seat auditorium and roof terraces.

The building sits in a bespoke basin and its lower sections were height-restricted by law, but those towering sails attracted opposition for being entirely out of character with the surrounding parkland. Eventually a change in planning regulations was required from France's National Assembly to allow the project to go ahead. Primary among the Assembly's justifications was that the museum would be "a major work of art for the whole world" – a statement that implicitly recognized Paris's reduced importance as a global hotbed for the creative arts and its efforts to redress that balance.

Opposite. Fondation Louis Vuitton, 2014.

But although the Fondation had its share of plaudits, it attracted brickbats too. For the plain-speaking Peter Buchanan, "The contrast between the diaphanous sails and the lumpy building proper is almost suggestive of butterflies hovering over a turd." Certainly, the structural contraptions on the rooftop – necessary to support those "diaphanous sails" – add obstructive clutter. Its appearance, which one critic described as a "cat's cradle", was evocative of Gehry's 2008 Serpentine Pavilion in London's Hyde Park.

In 1988, MoMA had included Gehry in its pivotal Deconstructivist Architecture exhibition, which had included the Gehry Residence. But although controversial (not least among his neighbours), that building offered a refreshing and witty riffing on vernacular Los Angeles architecture, inventing strategies to "intentionally violate the cubes and right angles of modernism" (to quote the exhibition's press release). But with Gehry's increasing fame and high profile came gilt-edged invitations to collaborate with exclusive clients: this is also the man who also designed a jewellery line for Tiffany that included a gem-encrusted collar priced at $750,000 and would go on to design a LVMH perfume bottle. For *The Guardian*'s Oliver Wainwright, the Fondation was proof that in the twenty-first century Gehry was becoming increasingly (and indulgently) self-referential and – granted a huge budget from LVMH's head honcho – had simply not known when enough was enough.

Of course, it's entirely possible that any initial *froideur* felt towards the building will pass. Much of Paris's most distinctive and innovative architecture, although lauded today, was initially met with bafflement, if not outright hostility. The Eiffel Tower was built as a showpiece of industrial engineering, but drew complaints from the get-go. Two years before the structure's completion, *Le Temps* published a petition from 300 creative artists – writers (including Émile Zola and Guy de Maupassant), painters, architects and sculptors – deploring it as "useless and monstrous".

Renzo Piano and Richard Rogers' inside-out exterior of the Pompidou Centre (1977) has long been a cherished part of the city's landscape, but that wasn't always so. When it opened, it was widely castigated ("hideous" – *The Guardian*). *Le Figaro* howled "Paris has its own monster, just like Loch Ness", while Kevin Power of *Arts Review* compared it dismissively to "a nuclear centre, or an oil refinery, or some early learning toy". The shocking otherness of both buildings outweighed their strengths as boundary-pushers that injected the city's historic architecture with a shot of modernity.

Gehry continues to be front and centre among purveyors of statement architecture. In 2021, for the tower that dominates the Luma Arles arts complex building in the south of France, he devised a crumpled, stainless steel-clad edifice rising from lower storeys that house a glazed atrium. Those reflective surfaces – set at a range of different angles and gently textured to provide a softer reflection – respond wonderfully to the changing light conditions. Again, art was a primary influence here – one artwork and one artist in particular. Vincent van Gogh lived in Arles for a spell and it was at a nearby asylum in Saint-Rémy-de-Provence that he painted his beguiling *Starry Night* in 1889. It was Gehry's contention that Luma Arles in the evening evoked something of the colours in Van Gogh's masterpiece. "The light is there", Gehry told Alain Elkann in 2021, "and I made it possible to see it the way that Van Gogh saw it."

His mission statement for the building also referenced the "visible, segmented strokes" with which Van Gogh described the contours of the local Alpilles mountain range in several paintings (including *Starry Night*), and which thus inspired the exterior cladding in another way. There were nods to the region's historic architecture too: that drum-like atrium through which visitors enter was influenced by Arles' famous amphitheatre.

An increasing number of Gehry's more recent commissions have a philanthropic impetus. His impressive Pierre Boulez Saal in Berlin – a concert hall whose modular design allows for a host of different configurations – was designed for Daniel Barenboim's West-Eastern Divan Orchestra. The ensemble – which comprises an equal number of Arab and Israeli musicians, as well as performers from other countries – was founded by Barenboim and the late Palestinian writer Edward Said. The hall's elliptical set-up allows an audience to surround the orchestra, creating a non-divisive space where spectator and performer are mere metres apart. Once again, Gehry collaborated with acoustician Yasuhisa Toyota to create the superb sound profile; both men worked pro bono. The ground floor and balcony form two ellipses, with different axes. The balcony is detached from the wall, allowing sound to move behind and above it, while the wooden surfaces (a honey-hued hardwood floor and Douglas-fir panels) invest the crisp acoustics with warmth.

That same humanistic instinct lay behind Gehry's decision to transform a one-time bank in Inglewood, Los Angeles, into a new rehearsal space for the city's youth orchestra, which offers tuition, support and instruments – all gratis – to 1,300-plus aspiring musicians from deprived backgrounds. To allow the sound sufficient space to rise before reflecting down again – crucial for optimizing its clarity – Gehry expanded the room's height by cutting into the floor and ceiling. "The YOLA students are getting the same stage dimensions and acoustics as the LA Philharmonic," he told *Architectural Digest*, proudly.

Less positively, Gehry's projects have long attracted unwanted attention for their environmental costs, and in the past he has attracted opprobrium for challenging contemporary criteria for sustainability. In 2010, he complained that many certificates awarded by the LEED (Leadership in Energy and Environmental Design) green-building rating system are "given for bogus stuff", adding that the expenses for sustainable construction "don't pay back in your lifetime".

That said, sustainability has increasingly become interwoven into working practice for contemporary architects, and Frank Gehry is no exception. Warmth and air conditioning for his acclaimed Richard B. Fisher Center for the Performing Arts (2000–03) at Bard College in Kingston, New York, is generated by geothermal heat pumps. The Dr Chau Chak Wing Building (2012–14; opened 2015) at the University of Technology Sydney business school in Australia, incorporated locally sourced bricks, timber that was reused or recycled, or taken from sustainable sources, and "green" concrete that incorporated waste from power stations as a substitute for some of its cement, alongside a host of other environmentally conscious features. (Gehry's trademark crinkled cladding, which some compared to a crumpled brown paper bag, was – like that of 8 Spruce Street – inspired by represent-ations of folded cloth in Renaissance paintings.) The CATIA software utilized by Gehry's office also plays its part in cost-effectiveness, allowing his team to produce more precise documentation that results in less confusion between architect and constructor, thereby saving on waste.

Above. Pierre Boulez Saal concert hall, 2017.

Meanwhile, his MPK 21 expansion of Facebook's Menlo Park campus in Palo Alto, California, USA (2017–18; an addition to the MPK 20 building, itself Gehry-designed), prioritizes natural light over its artificial counterpart via the use of plentiful glass, alongside rooftop solar panels and a water-recycling system.

The Fondation Louis Vuitton also utilizes recovered rainwater – something that Paris experiences in abundance. Once filtered, it can be used to clean the building's glass panels and façades, irrigate the terraces and flora, and replenish the site's basin. Ground-water tables help provide geothermal energy to maintain the temperature within the building. Shade from those sail-like canopies also helps reduce energy costs.

As for the environmental impact of building Luma Arles: "I respond to every fucking detail of the time we're in with the people we live with, in this place," he insisted to *Dezeen* in the year of the tower's construction, adding the slightly vaguer, "It's all taken into account as best I can." True, renewable sources supply a percentage of the building's energy needs, while the atrium makes energy savings by using natural ventilation. The interior cladding incorporates salt, algae and agricultural waste, all sourced locally. But the exact size of its carbon footprint remains uncertain and it's unlikely to be modest, given the sheer scale of the steel-and-concrete tower.

The self-confidence that enables an architect to challenge conventional perceptions can easily stray into hubris, especially when boosted by international acclaim and the courtship of prestigious, moneyed clients. When Gehry declares that the Luma Arles tower "makes it possible" to see the light the way Van Gogh did, is that objective fact or fanciful presumption?

Shortly after flipping the finger to a room full of Spanish journalists on that infamous occasion in 2014, he let rip with: "Every now and then ... a small number of people do something special. They're very few. But – my God! – leave us in peace!" Is that vanity or a straightforward demand by one of the world's leading architects to be recognized for his achievements?

Moreover, what price avant-garde subversion at a time of climate change and waves of refugees fleeing conflict zones? As global economic crises, pandemics and European war dominate the headlines, architectural extravaganzas with eye-wateringly large budgets are met with increasing scepticism in some quarters. "If you scroll back through deconstructivism's built legacy," Catherine Slessor complained in *Dezeen* in 2022, "you find no housing, hospitals, schools or transport infrastructure ... Instead, there is an abundance of posturing, theorising and showpiece art museums."

There's no sign of Gehry tempering his architectural vision any time soon. The Abu Dhabi Guggenheim on Saadiyat Island – first announced in 2006 but subjected to repeated setbacks – is currently scheduled to open in 2026 and will be larger than any other Solomon R. Guggenheim Foundation museum. It's a characteristically busy Gehry design, intercut with jagged extrusions, angular roofs and cubic structures. The conical metal entrance halls, which double as exhibition spaces, seem reminiscent of paper sheets scattered across an artist's desk, though they were directly inspired by the region's wind towers – another example of Gehry taking the time to tap into the local culture and traditions. Other aspects of its construction have seemed less sensitive, including concerns over the treatment of migrant labourers.

> Architecture, once the encompassing mother of the arts completed by sculpture and painting, and carrier of cultural significance and meaning, has become reduced to superfluous spectacle.
> Peter Buchanan
> *The Architectural Review*, 2015

Frank Gehry has produced some of the most talked-about and acclaimed buildings of the past half century. That he's also regularly pilloried for his designs can hardly surprise him: the project that marked his breakthrough – the Gehry Residence – received more than its share of flak alongside the praise. More than ever today, his extraordinary visions must face up not only to sceptical critics but also to the socio-political demands of our era. Does that put such an idiosyncratic architect out of step with the times? Or should buildings invested with greater humanity, whose fantastical appearance seem to have been plucked from a dream, and which at their best raise the heart and spirit – like a Michelangelo sculpture, or a Leonardo painting, say – always have a place in our lives?

Overleaf. Art Gallery of Ontario, Toronto, 2008.

[01, 02] Danziger Residence, Los Angeles, 1965; [03] O'Neill Hay Barn, San Juan Capistrano, 1968.

[04]

[05]

[04, 05] Davis Studio and Residence, Los Angeles, 1972; [06, 07] Gehry Residence, Los Angeles, 1978, and again in 1994.

[08, 09] Spiller Residence, Los Angeles, 1980; [10, 11] Indiana Avenue,
Los Angeles, 1981.

[12] Norton Residence, Los Angeles, 1984; [13, 14] Winton Guest House,
Lake Minnetonka, 1987; [15] Schnabel Residence, Los Angeles, 1989;
[16, 17, 18, 19] Vitra Headquarters, Basel, 1994.

340

[20] Chiat/Day Building, Los Angeles, 1991; [21] Golden Fish, Barcelona, 1992; [22] Frederick R. Weisman Museum of Art, Minneapolis, 1993; [23] American Center, Paris, 1994; [24, 25] Nationale-Nederlanden, Prague, 1996.

[29]

72 Neuer Zollhof

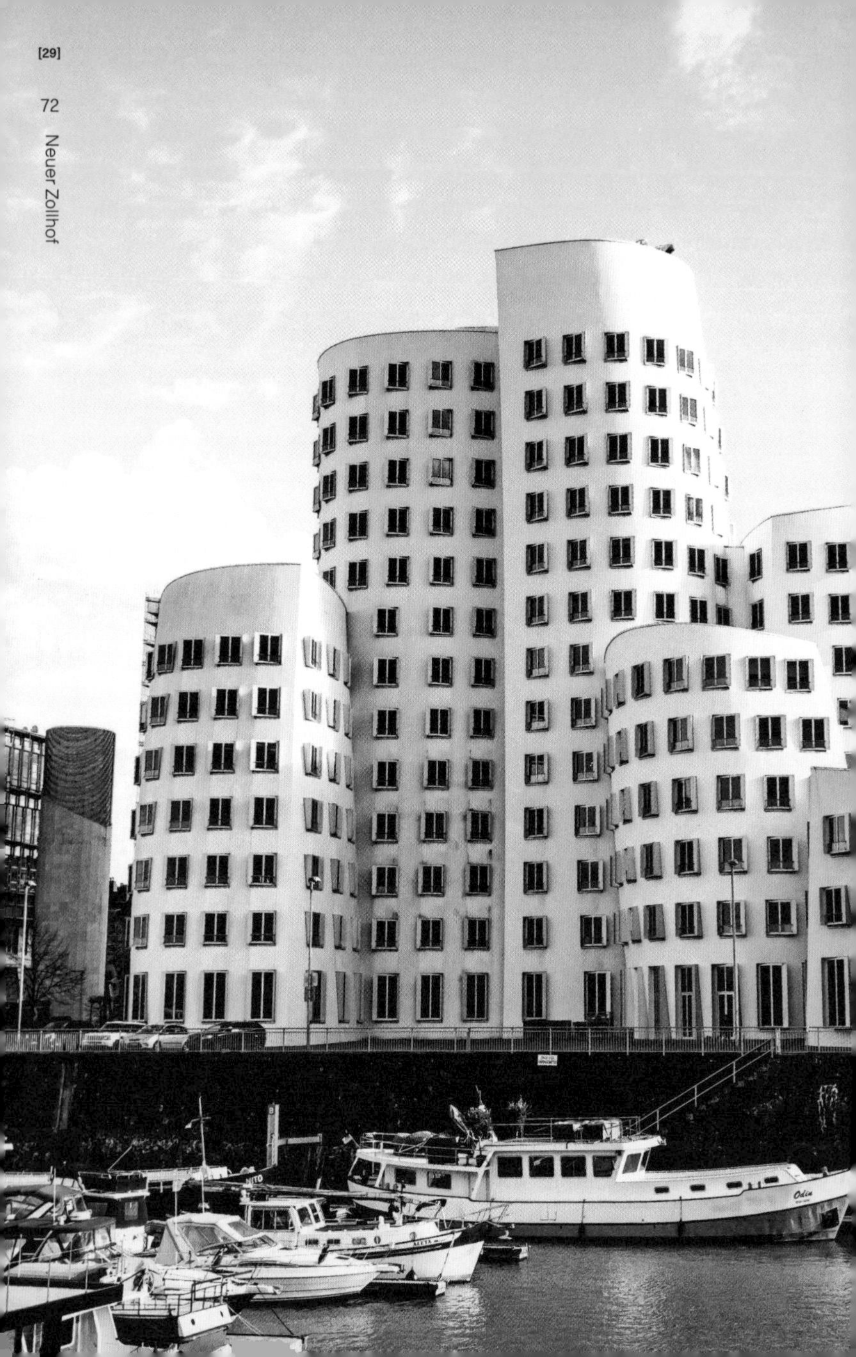

[26, 27, 28] Guggenheim Museum Bilbao, 1997; [29] Neuer Zollhof, Dusseldorf, 1998;
[30, 31, 32] MoPOP (Museum of Pop Culture), Seattle, 2000.

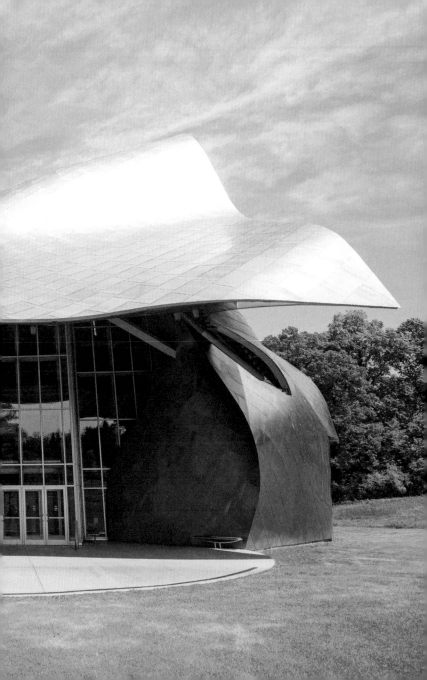

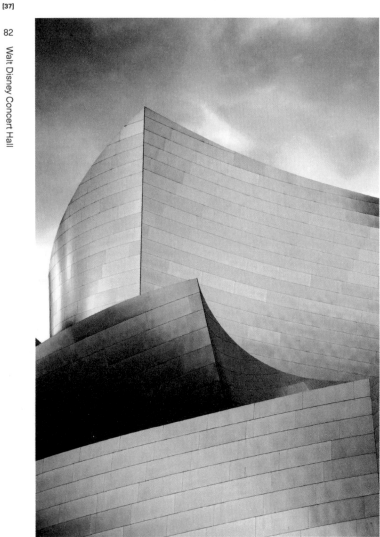

[33] Gehry Tower, Hanover, 2001; [34] DZ Bank Building, Berlin, 2001; [35] Peter B. Lewis Building, Cleveland, 2002; [36] Richard B. Fisher Center for the Performing Arts, New York, 2003; [37, 38, 39] Walt Disney Concert Hall, Los Angeles, 2003.

[39]

[40] Maggie's Centre, Dundee, 2003; [41, 42] Jay Pritzker Pavilion, Chicago, 2004;
[43, 44] Stata Center, Cambridge, Massachusetts, 2004.

[46]

[47]

[50]

[51]

[45] MARTa Museum, Herford, 2005; [46, 47] Marqués de Riscal, Elciego, Spain, 2006;
[48, 49] IAC (InterActiveCorp) Building, New York, 2007; [50] Serpentine Gallery, London,
2008; [51, 52] Art Gallery of Ontario, Toronto, 2008.

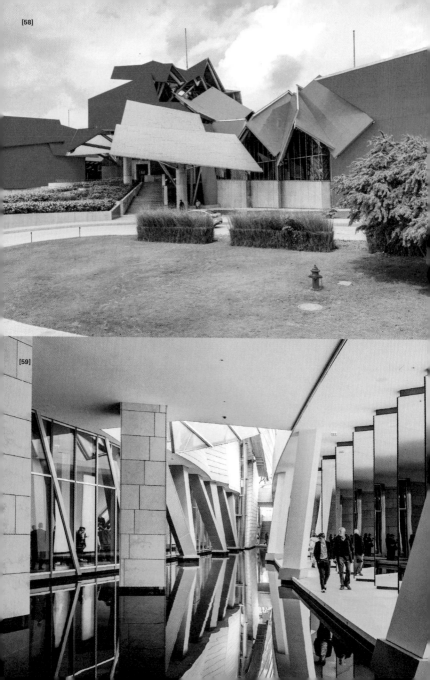

[53, 54] Cleveland Clinic, Las Vegas, 2010; [55] 8 Spruce Street, New York, 2011; [56] Opus Hong Kong, 2012; [57] New World Center, Miami, 2011; [58] Biomuseo, Panama City, 2014; [59] Fondation Louis Vuitton, Paris, 2014; [60] Dr Chau Chak Wing, Sydney, 2014.

[65]

[66]